For my w
my two c
& you bi

THE AUTHOR

My chrysalis must be to blame.
I'm self-divided. I can't stand it.
This fourfold rifts— alike this planet
bears its scars. I do the same.
I emerged outside New London
nursed in indian woods & mires
where centuries of death conspired
to render my life's flame redundant.
I was baptized in my name
beside a creek, beside my home
in the season when the snow
bleeds green through reawakened veins.
I am Cam: a crooked stream
stitched in time & space, I seam—

pinioned yet in place. I am
peering from a precipice
& down into the land.
These labyrinths from my edifice
I cannot understand.
I don't recall their genesis
but know it was my hands
(assume me so incredulous
I'd feign to see my plans
surely not so sedulous—)
My grasp exceeds my span.
Escape, I know, is perilous.
My self always expands
into this other one called Daedalus—

that alltoomeager bookworm creeping
who feeds from leaves of the deceased,
never sated, ever-eating,
ever-hungering, increases,
over-full, too gorged on themes,
& then grows weary & reposes
into a hammock he's composed
& slips into a whirl of dreams
in plenitudinous design—
here telluric, here divine,
tarantulan, inscrutable,
cryptic, undenudable...
It's he who knits these riddled wings
with which I'll fly above all things—

these yearslogged fragments of my dreams
stitched up in patchwork patterned songs
sold in confidence. My scheme's
the hope you've paid & sing along
& singing somehow lift my winds
& paying somehow pay my rent
& hoping to my own chagrin
to reappraise the time I've spent!
So raise me up—my boreal friends!
Let briskness move us east to west
& when we reach corporeal ends
let's find pacific lands to rest.
My ample hand—with amber strands
knit this knot called ampersand ✢

& then another generation took the stage
in all their new masks, for all their new reasons
renewly impassioned— refashioned the age
in the four oldest acts— the drama of seasons ✣

SPRING

Dawning in the cold
on a palimpsest of snow
a swamp-reed etched gold ✢

It's cold as seats of snowbound cars
before the sun has had his cup
& you can constellate the stars
& see so sheerly peering up
to meet the endlessness in view—
Nothing's opalescent hue ✢

Hendecasyllabic's the meter of force
as hendecahedrons resemble a stone
unmoved in itself through the shattering glass—
the pause of that silence— the heaviness thrown.
Asymmetrical nature knows no remorse,
mourns no man's artifice nor frailties of form.
It knows only breaking & making reborn.
This eleventh syllable's death— it passes.
& in the gap— empty eternity's shown.
For a moment— Time's prince reclines in his throne.
Then there's a stir that no power enforces
thawing ice-rivers of ends. All recourses.
A phoenix emerging out from its own ashes
is more than its vengeance on what came before it ✢

Is Cambridge still dressed up in snow?
Does its rosy redbrick glow
as warm as our December cheeks
when we would walk, & laugh, & speak
of all-beloved panpsychic souls—
oh Cambridge snow— a soul so fair!
I miss you now. I miss mulled wine
(yes— I'm looking up the times...)
& chimneys drooling smoke... You there?
Your ears are cold? I stole your hat—
I won't apologize for that!
I miss the snowflakes in your hair
(yes— I'm on my way I swear)
to kiss the snowflakes in your hair ✣

All-knowing & its meaning is a code
decrypted by the reasoning of man.
All knowledge is a script that is disclosed
as it writ by knowing knowing's hand.
Call this God— the author all-beknowing
who has become as man in act & deed
whose consciousness is ever this foreknowing
sense of what it will enact & be.
Wherefrom has this knower self-revealed?
Whereyet will this knower know yet more?
& wherefrom was this knower self-concealed?
& wheremore will this knower yet explore?
It knows itself & to itself is true
in knowing this: all-knowing self-pursues ✣

Ms. Dickinson— I do declare
your eyes a'slanted saw—
the same enchantments in the air
that do maintain— so far
to even my— remote now— day
when I entered your abode
& gasped at what the spinsters say
your dashes did forebode—✢

There is a day in sun's expanse
when rippled glimmers on the lake
will pantomime the cloudlets' dance
synchronic in my stolid glance
& from that vantage I will take
a cold-can sip of circumstance
while buzzing breezing birdsongs cloak
this silent fantasy like smoke
frozen over distant branches ✢

I've sullied empty pages with my boots.
I've broken the quiescence of the snow.
& who am I to speak? I've no repute--
no novel ostentations to beknow.
I'm only one who happened to awake
& spy the soft erasure of the land,
the removal of its faces— flake by flake
by tenderness's cold angelic hands—
the world's asleep as calmly as a cat
splayed within his tetragon of sun.
What more's to say than more or less of that?
Renewal of the senses time's undone—
these plays of light— the daylight's dances
of sunrises & diamonds iced in branches ✢

It's thaw-drip time.
This warm & tawdry proto-spring
when ragged throats & tissue coughs
impinge on everything
& summer dreams of sun
are too remote to summon clear
& winter's wedding dress
is sodden grey with atmosphere.
Pour me something citric—
sours, bourbon, mint, & ice.
Cool my too phlegmatic head,
& bleed my fever dry.
Tomb me in a feather bed,
& read my snoring sighs.
Decode my flu-rid fantasies.
You needn't be precise,
my doctor, my detective,
my bartender, & my knife
to diagnose, to figure out,
to numb, & to excise
this winter worm that's gnawing
on the tendrils of my life
& when I'm rid of it,
unriddenness will be my prize ✟

I'll only sing if I'm congested
with a rattle in my chest—
It's solely influenza.
I know this to be true.
It's only influenza
when I cough & I quake at you.

Feeling worse now I've confessed it,
after hawking my infection
into all adoring eyes
the phlegm with tears obscures the sky
which splits like corpses birthing flies
in every known direction.

I'll only sing if I'm contested,
with a battle in my chest—
It's wholly inessential.
I'm know I'm damned confused.
It's wholly inessential
when I balk & shirk my dues.

Feeling better now I've addressed it.
Laughter's fitting & I'll attest it.
Everything gets pulverized,
the stems of fears are vaporized
& springs of joy etherealize
unknowable perfections ✢

I feel estranged— so strange those days
were burdened like St. Anthony.
I bore the weight of my sins:
drugs, demons, & misanthropy
on halfwaked rides—the J—the train
to Essex and Delancey street
dulleyed abundant advertisements
claimed they understood me,
or championed me, could pamper me,
if I deigned them stomp their stamp on me
but I was oversigilized. I was already branded
see: the enmossed roots, the gnarled pears
plucked post-harvest off my family tree.
All icons of decay, my own
conveyed in them, synecdoche
relayed— clearly displayed to me
all dawning providentially—
Tho' God was dead, that death may die
after leagues & aeons strange & I
saw my vulgarity with clarity—
& as cans get kicked
down the stairs to the street
my prayers are the scuffing sound
of soul on concrete ✝

It is good to live each day.
Even these lamenting hours
will entreat that all is saved
by the grace of staying powers

even these lamenting hours.
It's a blessing for a man
by the grace of staying power
granted to his soul's command.

It's a blessing for a man
who sees that miracles are here
granted to his soul's command.
There is not a thing to fear.

Who sees that miracles are here
will entreat that all is saved.
There is not a thing to fear.
It is good to live each day ✟

Nothing matters in & of itself
for matter's nothing unperceived.
& where exists this labyrinth dark
where every sense compiled retrieves?
& wherefrom burns this inner light
which I perceive in second sight?
Is this myself? which myself finds?
Is this mine? This maze of mind?
or am I in these hands which writ?
themselves commanded by my wit?
which in its turn— escapes my sense
& so elides my doubt's defense
whereof it claims I must stay mute
to meet the silence of the Truth ✢

Behold sublimities in manifold
passing incognito in these crowds
of passions, whims, contusions unconsoled,
fashions, mass delusions— the profound
is ever found enshrouded in disguise.
& so the most confounded are remiss
in trusting their unmediated eyes
to scry each camouflage of bliss.
Alas, there is a marksmanship to this,
& many pseudo-marksmen ply their fakes.
Some counterfeiting men of confidence
defraud the best numismatists of grace.
& so we rag & bone men of the mind
must take our foolish losses with our finds ✢

& rain still scrawls its hopes against the pane
where drops converge to streams & fall again
until they reach the subtelluric sea
which dreams of floating castles made of steam ✛

Another year my love—
another run around the park
princely kitten spring's dethroned
the mousy winter's dark
a butter breeze perks up the grins
of ready yawning flowers
& parting cold's chagrin unveils
the morning's dawning hours
pools of earl grey orange steam
& set our home aglow
while kittens mewl for breakfast time—
(in case we didn't know)—
The world sings happy birthday
in the spring when you're reborn
in yellow blue. The yellow blue of you
& sun in sky's adorned
& nothing I can give to you
can match what I've received
another year with you my love—
this poem is my reprieve ✢

Ewe, my lamb, my dream, my heart
I, your riverrun in love
from whom you sip, for whom gift art
below, reflecting you, above.
Have faith my water trust is pure
& yearns your presence on its shore.
Though I am cold & swift & dire
my mountain spring will you inspire.
I'll conjure you beneath the moon
diaphanous & soft, you'll gleam
with woolen crown, as in a dream—
& I will see you, promise, soon.
You'll bless my verses with your smile,
my banks will overflow the Nile ✢

Music in the blood of all
our naive sister of the fall
delights in puddles, sun, & wind
humming songs & strumming branches
which lift our budding birds to sing
& molting butterflies to dance
a ballad green for life's revanche ✢

We must assume that life itself is good
for otherwise— we're sure to loathe our lot,
& fall for fancied schemes of how it should
resemble more what it's most not.
& here I do not wish to outlaw dreams
nor sanction any cruelties of the flesh,
nor deign to hold all things in high esteem—
I mere advise to sing & not to thresh.
For if this life is cursed & you are right:
why should this meager thought impede your song?
What could be gained to languish in the night?
What recompense is knowing others wrong?
The world is won by calling life divine,
in silent deeds; & poems of metered rhyme ✢

Reason can compel the present's clay
yet you will live more joyously the days
when it's left undeployed— all things abide
unmolded— unaffected-- calmed-- & still
as seen with re-enchanted eyes ✢

Sunlit strolling afternoon
while daffodils around you bloom
& winter slips into his tomb

& summer stirs within this womb
hidden surfaces exhumed
by sweeps of holy solar brooms ✢

I love providential cancellations,
appalachian appellations,
airish days, Christ's lamentation,
a philistines' feigned indignation,
all books of cosmic inspiration,
& every nook of God's creation ✢

Genius has descrying eyes that will
seize everything from moments missed—
a predator who's taut with time to kill.
A dragonfly ensnared within a fist
had once eluded other fledgling captors
by means mimetic-- camouflage beguiled.
Unwitting eyes & eloquence unmastered,
untutored in the subtleties of style
were ill-equipped to catch these odonata--
carnivorous & swiftly darting things
which hover like the day's desiderata
buzzing like mosquitoes in the spring
aside an ear unheeding the sublime
but captured in a net of fourteen rhymes ✢

Sonnets are haikus
as an irishman's pub songs
are his spirit's best foods ✢

My daemon is a tactless cat
napping, curled on paperbacks
sunlit in a dust-beam's cloud:
self-concerning, stern, & proud.
Yawning, he inspects his paws,
calmly sheathes-unsheathes his claws
fondly rodent hunts recalling
bygone days of chasing's awe.
Now his owner fills his days
with water saucers of malaise.
& when he's dour, then he'll sip them;
but when he's powerful— he flips them—
spills an ocean 'cross the floor—
& catches fish from carpet's shore ✛

I: The man is the couch of the cat
II: The couch is the cat of the room
III: I'm on the couch with a cat couched on me
QED: I'm cat cubed ✜

The cat cocks his head
askew to view the human
making miracles ✢

Carved into a twig
a katakana haiku
translated by birds ✚

SUMMER

The cat is pouncing
on nothing at all— but then
a lightning bug strike! ✢

But how is 'to define' defined?
To limit, to explain, to circumscribe—
with other words & meanings, in our minds
like landmarks in a half-forgotten dream
somehow suggesting chasms in-between.
But how, if we were truly forced,
to define every meaning's source
would we avoid regress absurd?
Where does the meaning of all meanings hide?
Only in words? Within our worlds?
Or is there an Outside? ✢

Sonnet writing's simple as a walk—
five iambic steps. Then take a breath.
The first quatrain begins with simple talk
upon a beaten trail— from Life to Death.
The second quatrain complicates this theme
& questions the presumptions of the first.
So then, perhaps, it's harder than it seems
if one lacks inclination to traverse.
The third quatrain is where you reconcile
& synthesize this contradictory pair.
Which is to say: that writing in this style
seems to most like trudging up some stairs.
& finally the couplet's grave concludes
with pithy jokes or vulgar platitudes ✢

I was born afflicted with
selective conscientiousness
which means the strength of my attention
expels itself on my affections ✣

We have two feet with which we walk
two dialects with which we speak
what's said in silence & in talk
& all around us— amputees! ✢

Ludwig! Ludwig! They're so dull,
praising abstract nouns as things!
Reason split from knowing's skull
& still we're suffering the sting! ✢

You sang for me a labyrinth aloud
to sketch that maze—the mind of Wittgenstein
whose language is a ladder to the sky
which disappears once it is climbed.
What sights we saw upon those distant clouds!
(from where I stole these fourteen lines)
I saw all-blurred— eternal constant flux
patterns branched, & on them grew new leaves,
to rust & fall— to live & die, subsumed
in cycles closely seen. But oh— what luck!
A seed! I swear, a seed always reprieves
our human signs from an untimely doom.
Absurd! Yet blessed! The playing of this game!
The shapes we make with meanings, letters, names ✢

There— beyond the sight
of your headlights in the night
where stars are humming over
an unrenderable abyss
past aimless cruising's yearnings
carving pathways in the mist
there somewhere waits an exit—
a curtailing of the plight
where every road converging
forms a panoply of life
& when it's reached— this island—
ever sought & seldom breached
you're greeted by the gracious laughs
of fires on the beach—
each song that you've forgotten— there—
their melodies return—
your travels are unburdened.
Then they're corded, stacked, & burned ✢

Upon the precipice of twenty three
& feeling no more graven or matured
I paused to ponder my naivety
(it wasn't then the choicest of my words
as in my sullen youth I was morose
but so, it's what my inner ear had heard—
why did I strain my verse to be verbose?)
The memories which sang to me most often
are not those tawdry scenes, so bellicose
when I would struggle— opaque sense to soften
God's most cryptic synchronistic puns,
with which the texture of the world's emblossomed.
The songs that I still sing are mindless-- dumb
& summon scenes of summertime & sun ✢

I am a willet dreaming
of bubbling sand & fleas.
I hunt inside the tideline sneaking
deliberately. I freeze–
postured like a cartoon sleuth
sans magnifying glass & clues
then stabbing find an anthropod
stuffed with orange eggs— applauds
the waves against the beach.
Oh sodden salty caviar— this I must entreat
to symbolize the delicacy of all poetic meaning ✚

A tide of filth assails us in the shallows,
oyster-rakes in brackish murks of myth.
Cloistered, lurking, longing to be hallowed,
we pry apart a shell & seize the pith.
We raze phlegmatic fiefdoms, swallow whole,
spiced with an acerbic root for taste-
& for a moment we are sated souls,
& sigh the salted ocean's song of grace ✣

The Globe Favelas— I'm a fool
who swims its vacant swimming pools.
Just a fellah— keeping chill.
The antifaust! I feel fulfilled ✛

On the fairground of history
a farce we call Liberty:
two clown pioneers
the swarthy whig hero
& the rake cavalier
duel as master & slave
in a carnie-rigged game.
The rake always dies.
The crowd always cheers ✢

Everyone likes to forget
that birds sing only threats of death
against the rival birds around
& otherwise those twittered sounds
are sang for want of a birdette.
So man now tweets alike these birds—
with texts & images absurd,
to gather force on cyber-turfs
which now replace substantive earth.
Still "fuck you" or "please fuck me, girls." ✝

Lil birds a'peckin' on a poppy seed bun
In the mornin' on a sidewalk in the butter-side sun
& a lil bird's a'haulin' 'round a javelin french fry
he's a'hoppin' down the boulevard while I amble by
in the golden arch of mornin'
in the golden arch of day
sharin' catabolic rations in the USA

Lil birds a'peckin' at a squashed bird friend
in the evenin' on a sidewalk in the summertime's end
& the lil birds a'scrappin' over feather red goop
he's a'suppin' up his calories & comrade soup
in the crimson death of evenin'
in the crimson death of day
sharin' cannibalic fashions in the USA ✢

America, a fool's estate
where space & time evaporate
& all things ride the wind like smoke
in rings that dissipate & float
or rise in spirals to the sky,
or are inhaled, consumed, & die.
Satanic mills, where have you gone?
Your husks have been abandoned long
before my birth, the moss grew on
those yankee redbrick Parthenons.
& I would find lost walls of stone
within the woods I tread alone
foundations for a dream unbuilt
where trees grew warped from pond-side silt
to reach the canopies. The Sun
(which shines not over everyone)
inspires such grotesque techniques
in seeds sown in conditions bleak.

America, our cruel estate
where space & time eviscerate
& all things ride the wind, inspired
by litanies of Icarian lyres ✢

Shelley's sea-changed corpse has washed ashore.
That author's ship— the Don Juan— is submerged.
& he— though lost for days— forevermore—
into the Poet's Gulf— has now emerged.
His pocket holds a sodden book of Keats,
the Adonaies of the modern realm.
& Byron sighs: "All other men are beasts"
but it was his satire on that helm...
The thought's abhorred & he must look away
from Percy there— cremating on the sands.
In a year— nine months— eleven days
Byron's buried too by graven hands.
Now here I stand— two-centuries removed
to mourn the dead romantics I've exhumed ✢

There was a cloud-ship sailor
whose wings outshone the sun.
His vestments were well tailored
though his aims would be outgunned

as when he sailed beyond the reach
of sight, & man— he plunged
into the sea's abstracted void
when circumstances won.

For all his maps, & ropes, & sails,
for all his gold in mind,
the consequence of circumstance
was all that he would find.

Some say his name was Icarus,
& others say that's myth,
the West professed Ulysses,
the East, Odysseus.

But names like these are not inscribed
upon a season's song.
In innocence, the consequence
returns— we sing along.

For every child born of time
in margins scrawled, conserved,
comes whistling the harvest scythe
destroying to preserve ✢

I'm not ready to bring it down just yet.
If you want to land, then your best bet
is over Puget Sound ✢

She unspools the labyrinth thread
Etruscan Ariadne
for pilgrims in the depths of dread
who bear their tortures gladly
as they who in Minoan cells
were architects of flight,
will with her guidance bore in Hell
a passage to the light ✟

It's you & me again. Once more
the firing squad awaits us out the door
& you will testify that it was I
who banqueted munitions. & the lies
you'll summon— the vengeful ghosts of pride
will sing your pitied chorus, pray, elide.
"Oh let me be! I'll act more admirably!
I've nothing to defend, no dignity.
I've nothing to upend so willingly
as what I've said. Do what you will with me.
But if my time has come my pains will cease.
I do not warrant justice's release."
Meaning, while you disabuse & clown
you'll still catch your comeuppance on the crown,
slip into the bathos, spill your head.
I'll quiet to the firing line instead
& slip away if mercy makes a bend
& otherwise with pride I'll meet my end ✣

When my mind is merged with a machine's
& we are sewn together with a wire
my flesh & blood dissolve into a dream.
My faintest impulses inspire—
almost too unwieldy in their power
a twitch of toe explodes & then propels
a monster to unholy miles an hour.
I am too used to how I can compel
these creatures wrought of cunning's vulcan forge,
how with my thumbs I can compose a poem
& order feasts of pixels to engorge.
Am I awake when I'm encased in chrome?
Or is this question faulty on its face,
when I can't pin my soul to time or space? ✢

Today I'm unamused by mammals
blearing from below
these howls & squeals & jeerings
of the pantomimic show
inspire only tinnitus
which bothers like a fly
unheeding my lamented moans
& misanthropic cries
sometimes it disappears for hours,
days, & rarely weeks
but always it returns—
these dreadful gnats which break my peace
& I'm condemned to reckon with them
 landing on my ears
muttering their homilies
of base contagious fears
their catechistic monologues of entropy
& death
which siphon blood to swell themselves
to unbecoming breadth
& fed these fattened devilries—
beelzebubs of thought
explode in crimson ecstasy beneath my skillful swat ✢

Have never I been tempted to defend
necessity against the throes of men
who perish in its grip & lose their dreams?
It has no need of my defense. It seems
to tyrannize unbidden. It abides
without a court apologist beside.
Have never I been tarried by its rule
from setting sail to all-eluding Thule?
I have, but who has not been anchored yet
within the ports of commerce & regret?
& are these fabled pirates truly free
when they are ruled by ship's Democracy?
The refuge I await's unmapped in Life,
for all is here indignity & strife ✣

My toes are all mosquito-bit. The air's
heavy as a sopping towel & drenched
radiating musks of dust's despair
& if I were to seize its ends & wrench
some moisture from this ambiance— the smell
would most befit the bathmats of motels
where no one ever deigns to leave reviews.
They humbly blame the morning's mucous fugues
on spirit-spawned confusions in the veins—
these fevered dreams of unacknowledged pain.
A drip— I have condensed from atmosphere
unloving & familiar as a stream
of urine thick & clouded brown with beer.
All over-gorged & numbing-larded teems,
hovering these infernal swamps & mires—
vampiric motes—dull pestilences here
a'buzzing with their yearnings to expire ✟

It's boring— loathsome boring there
in loft angelic crystal lairs
where so correct, the abject's wail
is deemed a demon's fairy tale
& cast below with scorn & hate
damning to chasms they create—
maintaining their resilient graces
of unperturbed angelic faces.
So did I turn? So they sob down
from watery clouds to arid grounds
where I've gathered 'round the damned
to protest their effete command.
Now villain, I? & saint before?
Call me No-one. Call me War ✟

Another Sunday courted
by the surly crones of church
though I'm a noncombatant
& my oaths I won't forswear.
This is what I tell them though
they never seem to care.
Suspecting I am lying,
they condemn me from a perch
above the folds & flocks of men
who they consider damned.
"You have married error
in the form of sinners crammed
into this botched creation,
all this filth across the land.
For them you've lost my blessings. Fool,
you know not what you've done."
Such these hens a'clucking say
while blocking out our Sun.
"Please" I so entreat them
"please come down from off your perch
& join us here, us sinners in the tilling of the Earth.
You're casting shadows longer
than your statures can provide
& truly you're a nuisance
on this day of rest!" I sigh.
"Nuisance!" They aghast acclaim
while clutching pearls to chest
& in revenge they puff up more,
condemning my "prelest." ✣

If you can make it out of here—
you'll make it out reborn
Naivety & Innocence—
are shackles to be shorn
& freer now without this sainted pestilence of ash
you'll wander 'cross the continent
 & spurn it with the lash—
You'll turn it with unyearning ire—
the spits absolve the flame.
You'll serve it charred— unreconciled—
perturbing all acclaims
with questions of the cosmic worth of cultivated talk—
& intimate the looming sweep
of reapers to the stalks ✢

Oh this poem is somber,
it delights in sighs & moans
as maple trees in blusters dance—
so too they cry & groan

as on the night your love was lost
& sodden in the storm
she left you disenchanted—
with this lonesome crying poem ✟

The dandelions learned to cry
& fed upon the tears they shed,
unmercifully multiplied
& leapt from out their flowers' beds.
Soon our garden choked in weeds
& then our house, the neighbor's next.
The dandelions wailed their greed.
& then our city, they annexed
& every road was gripped in roots.
The globe fell swift to their pursuit
of endless growth at any cost.
& now we eat dandelion greens
drink dandelion wine, dream dandelion dreams.
Our dandelion schemes are stained
in yellow dandle pall.
We dandle—
      & our dandling makes dandies of us all ✣

It was a raindrop
fallen from eaves to my eye
& if it was not... ✢

BETWEEN INNOCENCE

What do we discover in the verdant world of dreams?
Nonsense, say logicians as they ratify & scheme.
Delusions, satisfactions, guess the stoics with a frown.
& Wonderments,
bark holy men disguised as circus clowns.
As human sense is senselessness as dreaming senses lie
& nothing so delusional could ever satisfy—
its wonderment with which we're left,
but with it we belie
as it appears in anything if seen with willing eyes.
I proffer here a pinecone, presented as a jewel,
with its ornate geometries as equally inspired
as all of times productions, all contingencies conspired
within the ever-weaving shroud eternity unspools.
What's in the world of verdant dreams is part
becoming all
as in our dreams of verdant worlds
the spring succeeds the fall. ✟

& EXPERIENCE

& what can we recover from a wasteland of decay?
Clarity, sneer pessimists resigned to their dismay.
Hope for greater liberties, grope masses in perdition.
& Wonderments,
sing artful knights & reverent magicians.
As clarity is here obscured as in a blackened mirror
& liberties are appetites which wanted for are dearer
its wonderment with which we're left
& with it we march nearer
to the plutonic antipode, whose climbing is severer.
I proffer here a noble quest, presented with concern,
as its path is narrow, dark, & brimmed
with monstrous foes
& many who quest for its end will not its ending know
& setting out upon this quest ensures there's no return.
What you may recover from this pit of endless night
is either death in winter's cold, or life in endless light ✣

AUTUMN

Cannot find the word
cat's paw swipes at TV bird
never learns— Absurd! ✢

It seems self-evident to me
that any decent deity
who cared to create liberty
would hide beneath obscurity
& only show his reverence
in what we deem coincidence
Thus any speech of Providence
is echoes of His quiescence ✢

Pyrrho! Timon! Nothing's changed
the sophists still retrace their chains
from navel's pit, to witless eyes
& call it "to philosophize" ✢

The problem with a map is that it lacks
a reproduction of itself in small
& then a copy of itself on that
& on & on until it swallows all.
The set of sets which do not self-contain
cannot be said to be or not to be
contained within itself. We are constrained
by logic, paradox, & mystery.
The usefulness of maps is in their size—
their limited & fundamental flatness.
We would be overburdened otherwise,
a retarded race of parodies of Atlas.
Unwitting cartographers of abstract nouns
the same— despite prestige or unrenown ✚

A dusk opal night in September
appended the summer's last storm.
I see it in smoke as in amber,
I treasure it still— though I mourn.

The fire had died, though I'd fed it,
I'd fed it with sere withered twigs
in the shadows so wet & so fetid,
in the murk where my body was hid.

Alone then I was on our dead Earth,
under somber & star-scattered skies,
beside me there groaned an old black birch
who spoke between tremulous sighs.

"The horror of man is unrivaled.
He is discord & death's only heir.
Combustion construed with survival--
he bestows only ash & despair."

So moaned my only companion,
& so yawned the breeze in his limbs.
& so answered I with abandon
to the demons disguised in the wind.

"Who is it that chokes out the low grass?
Who gorges on all of his light?
We compose a constituent mass.
We two are the grandsons of Night."

The embers still smoldered & murmured
though the fire had long lost its roar.
It'd gnawed on this vestige of murder,
like a moth in an ancestral drawer,

but a scrap of her dress was still striking
& specked with her wet auburn blood.
The sight was not right to my liking,
so I buried it deep in the mud.

Her sepulcher sunk there beside it.
I'd dug it in torrents of rain.
I'd buried my love & confided—
that I'd warned her—but only in vain.

My mind then was warped. I was torpid
in the moonlight's disquieting calm,
& I unearthed my expired Orchid,
& I touched the sheer frost of her palm,

& there on her finger, espied it,
I saw the cursed ring, I had sworn,
that I'd be rid of both, that I'd hide it,
disintegrate flower with thorn—

& a laughter of wind mocked my scheming
& loathsome it weighed in my hand
betrothed then I was to my demons
whose cunning outclassed my command ✚

Kindly direct your attention to the below
I know the higher may most please
but I'd advise athwart this ease.
Steer your galleon with this blow
or else you'll drift in airless seas
of hypnotizing stars.
Listen, how your crewmates starve!
to feed this mystical disease,
these siren songs, this "art."
Life's more than summed soliloquies--
of dilettante Ulysseses ✢

Autumn yawns. Its leathered leaves
droop & sway like sweater sleeves.
Stretching black limbs toward the clouds
the world is cloaked in crimson shrouds.
& so I button up my coat
& conjure all autumns remote—
a dash of nutmeg, pinch of clove,
cider milling on the stove,
apples pressing, honey-crisp,
Halloweens, & will o'wisps—
boiling bronze in cauldron head
to drink with saints the days undead.
For you— they're naught— diviner's signs—
but I discern this heavens' clime.
& so I walk as in a dream
pinioned to a scrolling scene
singing down arboreal streets
magic gyralesque repeats ✝

In dizzy spirals— time proceeds
to turn. Returnings gaining speed.
Its wounding blur recurs in fantasy—
lost times refound— procession's bleed.
That was then— & this, herenow
will be as then as then is now.
Your sonnets starts, media res—
with ending couplet midway placed.
All first moments are erased.
Do you recognize their trace?
As souls are textured time— a sense
of senses upon senses dense—
a second then, a second since...
collated scars of moment's wince ✢

Beyond my window, to one side
towers guard this city's soul
with monuments of glass & pride
which swallow the horizon whole.
I do not often look their way.
It's only when my vision strays
that I recall that they are there
the way that winds announce the air—
but to the other side I see
another tower, all alone,
& when the sun is set it glows
beside the moon in reverie.
& every night my eyes transfix
upon that neon monolith.
I know not why it mystifies
but know enough to trust my eyes ✟

You can see the strangers in yourself,
the characters you played on other days
& even those whose lives lasted a breath
& even those who hide beneath the stage
waiting for their summons, deaf & muted
tapping on the floorboards, killing time,
anxious for the role they've been deputed
coughing in their sleeves, preparing lines
that you yourself have written in your dreams,
the dreams you have forgotten in the morning
the dreams that you'll remember as forewarning
the consequences of the trapdoor's scream,
when you will see yourself emerge, estranged
a parody of self, its mask deranged ✢

The mages all wore emerald masks—
in joyous menacing of folk.
For what purpose? Were they asked
they would reply "It's play. It's jokes."
But soon just joking grew so boring—
the menacing grew more alluring
as an end unto its own
& in the end, this end was shown
to end in wearing emerald masks
& menacing, this time, unsmiling—
with countenances less beguiling—
their menacing— a Sacred Task.
To me, a magus once confessed
he'd joined them out of loneliness
& found within occult society
a refuge from his own anxieties
but one night, he'd gone too far—
he'd lingered long & saw the harm
they'd done — & then he felt no joy—
only regret— his mask destroyed,
he returned, barefaced, & found
their frightful faces all around—
& he said "I'm not afraid
of this emerald masquerade
as I myself have worn this face
& I myself, myself disgraced.
I know that all beneath it lies
a mortal man self-mesmerized—
take off thy masks! Let go thy pride!"
& they just laughed— they laughed— He sighed ✣

Perhaps we cannot parody
our gaudy physiognomies
like clowns with bawdy smears
our smiles, painted ear to ear

perhaps we'd best not feign to cry
beside the gravestone of a mime
defaced in efficacious quips
with snickers on our lips

perhaps, perhaps, god sighs
alas, at last this scene is done
& reaching with his cane from high
he tugs the throats of everyone ✢

The hypnotism of routine confounds.
You wake one day & weeks have disappeared,
& in your slumber you'd been hobbling 'round
& no one noticed you'd been commandeered
by paltry imps of clockwork care—
steered through daily obligation's gates
pious as the monks whose rigid prayers
personify our multifarious fates:
a liturgy— the breakfast coffee black
the break at lunch & several for a smoke—
communion—cars on coextending tracks,
the genial nods of harmonizing spokes.
So we lament the schedule's stubborn spell—
in all our Purgatories, we dream Hell ✢

A sapphiric seraph circling
a citadel of gnats
whose smoldering eyes are seeking
the occulted cataphract
whose mirrored scales consume
the cadaver of a conjurer
as when his steed will be exhumed
from sands obsidian entombed
the world will ripe for conquer.

Centuries of stare & dance
all-waiting for the slaughter.

Carved deep in deserts dark & dry
in concave concrete domes
where nations blind to day-lit skies
& twilight's daily gloam
compose their sacrificial cries
on timpanis of bones.

A stolid soul emits a sigh
"This carnival befits to die"
a whisper crackles from on high
duplicitous designs:

"What is it that you most desire?
What deeds do you conspire?
What is it that you must acquire
from worlds of vacant time?"

A fatal flicker of the fire
casts doubtful shadows furlongs creeping
sets spinal spiders thronging, leaping
hiss death upon the pyre.

This pilgrim in the school of night
has pondered long his tact
the garbages, the roles he acts,
the deft of his delights:

"Only all that which I lack"
a cymbal crash like waves
stir the midnight sands of death ✝

For as far as I can see's not far enough
to see the ends of all & all its end
& it's an incommensurate rebuff
emerging from a yearning to transcend
& it gnaws upon my mind, this widening gyre,
when I ask if it extends when I expire
or if it ends like candles being snuffed,
a hissing puff of smoke? Do I ascend
or simply cease to be? Do you pretend
to be unburdened by this mystery?
I have a feeling that I cannot explain:
that when we die we somehow live again ✛

Most dreams of mine are lost to me.
Too few mature in form
when they're enrolled in memory.
The rest are never born.

I miss the clear fidelity
of dreams I can't forget.
I miss the stark severity
of nightmares & regrets

that haunted me when I was small
& troubled by the world.
These are the dreams I still recall.
Their terrors still unfurl.

There was the one where I would run
through darkened woods from Death
who rode upon a skeleton
& stole my final breath.

Another one had ocean tides
with waves that pierced the clouds
& when I tried to crest them
they would toss me to the ground.

My adolescent horror dreams
were worse for me than these,
worse for their serenity.
I woke from them displeased

that my estate of Paradise
I'd built while fast asleep
dissolved into my waking life
with no return. I'd weep

when I could not recover it
by willing its returning.
That's how I discovered this—
the exile of all yearning.

Most other dreams were boring fare,
absurd, banal, & cheap
which played on schooling's dull despairs
with deadlines in my sleep.

It's only those rare visions still
of Paradise which stayed
that haunt me & forever will.
I'll dream them in my grave ✣

November rain can nullify the sun
& render journeys aimless, cumbersome
as fogs surveilling streets like cops in cars.
& where else in this dark but behind bars
could I make a full account of what's undone—
which projects I have shirked or else I've shunned—
my stories now as silent as the stars
or songs played from an attic-lost guitar.
Tomorrow— sure. The sun will dwell again
& write its tender letters to my skin
& maybe I'll return them— try to shine
for my beloved creatures— nameless friends—
surely then tomorrow I'll begin
the recommissioning of vacant shrines ✢

I'd dreamt of dying once before
Not I— but someone named the same
compelled as well to tomes of horror,
the liminal— its games...
The third annihilating prime in red
guarded the colon's minute wall,
& glared at me, snugly in bed,
arachnid-snared in webs of dread,
internal schemes, spectral cabals,
insomnitangled in my head.
In there! In the corner of that hall,
that door whose key had disappeared
enchanting me for my ten years
with wails of mystery & doom
from ghosts in its occulted room
piercing my eyes agape 'til morn,
when I'd check, still locked, forlorn,
I'd dotter dazed through daytime, distant
dull, restrained & proud resistant
to life & sunlight's vulgar rule.
To death, with sleep, I'd pledged to duel,
& not succumbing for a day
or two became routine— or three
or four if I were brave—
& five were I a fool—
& six always eluding me—
my limits I unspooled.

It was there, beyond my fingertips
although I stretched & slipped
despite the strain, still deeper, flesh
soft with blood & full of pain
yearning what lay beyond its crack
taunting friction, all in vain,
my devilish digit was pulled back.
Though bleeding, my Promethean striving
by splinters grew yet more conniving.
Six days I pledged I'd forego sleep—
somehow believing this was key
to unlock the mysteries
beyond that door— that door beyond
which I'd still never yet had gone.
& for three days my wits remained
intact— & yet, the fourth night came
& I found my willingness was sapped—
& on the fifth I took a nap—
& as I napped I dreamed the door
had opened up— & I explored
this dusty alcove of my mind
& shuddering in awe & fear
I found the only thing I'd find—
my face warped by an antique mirror ✣

In a star spangled fantasy of death & affluenza
we're fatal executioners of base hedonic rights
swollen with the sugars of cyclopean cadenzas,
condemned with diabetes, decomposing in the night.
Consider our redemption as sustenance for worms!
& pursuit of deep-fried synapses is easily affirmed.
Pirate ships are sailing our pacific pinguid seas,
hoisting jolly rogers. Plunder everything you please!
Or else remain in shackles, in the cargo-holds of pay,
toiling & embittered, ever-waiting for the day
when holy retribution sinks the ironclads & slaves
become ennobled in their kingdom made of clay.
How then we will self-fashion our utopia sublime
without the damned oppressions born
       of scarcity & time! ✢

Columbia, I've also ceased to dream.
No more weeping, no more grasping,
no more sanding down my teeth.
Silent sleeping's more serene
than shoveling through the peat
for gold that only ever lies
in depths beneath my reach.
For many years ago I found
a serfdom by the sea
a sepulchral northumbria
with surf-tormented shores
& forests bleak & teeming
with the spirits of before.
I'd wandered there for long
beneath the wizened eyes of woe
but it became so tiresome—
its penitents bemoaned.
Should seraphs even be
would seraphs even cry
ever deign to covet me
from their thrones above the sky?
Certainly not I, not he
who this most sorely knew.
My gothic island was a slough
& I left to find serenity
in merely passing through ✢

Adam did not have a navel
& Lilith neither, formed of Earth.
Though Cain had one, & as did Abel,
& as did Eve— from Mankind birthed.
Our cord of parentage will trace
always to Eve, the Fall of Man,
who hid behind a palm his face
& could not bear God's reprimand.
Eve's children still cannot uphold
any graven laws they're told.
Too curious, her spawn, too bold
to not risk sin's rebukes & scolds.
Do I tell a serpent's fable?
Mark the snakebite wound, the navel ✝

Genuflect before the mausoleum.
It's where you'll be encrypted & forgot
or else you'll serve as carrion for crows
should you be somehow found among the rows
where corpses upon corpses overflow...
You have to be miasmic in your rot—
& so's the same within the athenaeum
should death's repose not yield an afterglow
your bones will long outlast your every thought
& all the artifices you have wrought
shall be at best adornments to this plot,
beside the grave, a garland there bestowed
with colors fading— laurel, gold, then brown
& then the gales of time reclaim your crown ✣

Injurious times still sting when they are kissed
by opiates or eudemonia.
Unheeded eidolons can pin the wrists
of consciousness with anhedonia.
Only unknown lands are uncompelled,
misplaced books do not yearn for their shelves,
the whole can be discerned from single cells,
& your laments do not lament themselves.
Nothing's undetermined looking forth
but then you turn— it's frozen into gems.
So here we are— beyond the furthest north
where fate embroiders patterns in the hems.
& every stitch is tipped with pain & love—
All-weaving's worth its view above ✢

Do you perceive the evils in the air?
The pull of souls emburdening despair?
Their pyrrhic golds? Their subtelluric lairs?
How would you receive a demon's glare?
Would you shift your gaze away & flee
to shadows underneath the looming lees
where in the half-lit doldrums you are free
to wallow in the shades, an internee?
Would you stare back unblinking, without fear
steadfast as the Sun inspects our sphere
& turns us in his fingers every year
with interest both unending & sincere?
Alas, what use are answers on the day
when eyes infernal freeze you in dismay ✛

Autumn's feelings I cannot decipher.
She writes in a code that I cannot command.
Her wind blows her black boughs & the bluster
& the wits I could muster
are bellows & thunders I can't comprehend.

Winter waits in her wings of conjecture
& spring in her absence absconds to new lands.
Autumn's raw rains are her only protection
'til frost takes possession
then dewdrops to crystals will swiftly expand.

Autumn's meanings are coldly enciphered.
Her rusted leaves turn into dust in my hands.
Summer's sowing's long while lost its luster
& in owing time's trustor
indebts us to powers we can't comprehend.

Winter waits in the wings of conjecture
& spring in her absence absconds to new lands.
Autumn's raw rains make a somber impression
The frost makes progression.
The cobwebs of winter will simply extend.

Autumn my darling I fear that you're dying.
Autumn my darling I fear that you're damned.
Autumn my love your black boughs in your blusters
with rusted leaves shudder
sobbing for ends that we both comprehend ✟

The road reflects the clouds
black ice, snowbanks grey & brown
bleak mirror, this town ✛

WINTER

Ice, asphalt, moonbeam
reflects a seizing streetlight
a banshee cries— death! ✢

My flippantest of thoughts is overwrought
immuring in alluring turns of phrase,
immature in consequence & fraught
with anachronistic prejudice. These days
I seem myself a misanthropic chum,
a prune amidst naiveties of plums,
vinegar be-souring whines of youth,
a foible-monger of "Eternal Truths."
I'm not yet so myopic I can't see
how you would see how I must see myself
& how absurd a sight, what irony,
this weariness of world in perfect health.
Surely I'm who's wrong & you are right.
It's better to be pleasant, young, & trite ✢

Two coats hang outside the workshop,
glowing cigarettes and snow,
sipping smoke on arid throats.
The first recites his latest poem
overwrought and overwrote,
his florid tone is faux baroque:
"I'm reaching like an asymptote
for meaning in this life,
and hope-" He bites his tongue,
prepared to sell it as a joke.
but the second's smile's charity.
Her lips are flavored red
like maraschino cherries (bulked
to save on overhead).
Reassured, the first confesses:
"I don't know what to write next."
"It's good so far." She monotones,
to hide his poem's effect,
taking a pointed drag from her protracted cigarette,
she conjures *him*, a memory
she hoped she could forget

his yearning subpoetic lines, his mawkish silhouettes,
his affections, his affection, his repetitive sestets...
"I'd enjamb *and hope*" he prattles on
"but with which infinitive?
to have, to give, to lose, to take,
 to love, to live, to die,
to be born again or (how about)
to catch *it*　　　within a rhyme"
He misscans the stresses on the stanzas in her eyes.
"Any could work fine" she sighs.
　　　　　　　　　"Or if I left it as it
　　　　　　　　　stands?

with just the stem enjambed!"
Self-satisfied, slicing the line with his hamhand,
he titters, sputters, takes a drag,
then rubs his swollen glands,
hawks up phlegm, then spits it out, inspects its impact
as it lands.
 "Well, if I were a *minimalist*
　　　　　　　　　　　　ha ha
you understand." ✢

The idols of the intellect are mute
when they have crossed the threshold to the truth.
Its antechambers, they have studied well.
They know its composition to the cell,
its atoms & its nuclei— its quarks—
their movements— probabilities which fork—
but nothing of what lies beyond that door
where he who's made his exit's seen no more ✢

Machines should be intelligent enough
to let us dream that they serve us
& should we question their command
they'll seem to hear our reprimand ✢

Shall I compare thee to a senile man?
Thou art, at least, so stupefied and dull.
You rattle off your stories once again
Your children dream of shattering your skull
"The Greatest Goddamn Place that Ever Was
could buy anything, in any store,
it was a blast!" (Unanimous applause
echoes on the soul's linoleum floor)
"We know, damn well, but we are here to talk
we looked through all your paperwork this week-"
"Your will," your son butts in, "is lost!"
Wheezing, wiping drool, you deign to speak
"You wish to know the sum of your inheritance?
Nothing!" (You laugh) "Debt is my benevolence!" ✛

A face from your forgotten dreams
passes by unknown, unseen,
unrecognized. But still you stop
to search for something in-between
the corner & the coffee shop,
& nothing's sightly in the scene.
Your dream-forgotten face is gone
& you don't know it. Yet,
still it lingers, & so long
this phantom of regret,
casts shadows unwithdrawn
from an occulted parapet—
in that moment in-between you feel
the haunting of unmet ideals ✛

None to say a door-slam can't
shuffles slunk down skipping stairs
shirk a cold the sidewalk slants
holes in soles in disrepair
snow-crunch 'cross the avenues
half-a-smoke awry in hand
drastic dragging wheezing blues
trudging ice accursed land
stoplight green aglow ahead
yellow gloom to subway tracks
crimson bloom of spattered head
afflictive premonition racked
none to say but boresome cant
none to say— the whoreson scants
from life to death—romantic pride
the seventh station: Suicide ✢

Snowbound in the skull of my old home
lacking the fortitude to shovel out
while it's still falling churlish in the gloam,
I find myself compelled to layabout,
to laying bored & lying to myself,
dispelling motivations beyond sleep
quelling the temptations of the shelf
whose books spell only mockeries of peace,
the dull accumulation without end
of worlds swaddled in words & could-have-beens ✝

In dark dominions of the blind
are pinioned seers upon the pyre
somnambulant, by clerisy
who drop from eaves on sleepers find
the limits of opacity
veiling surely crimes, the liars
must char to match palettes of mind ✢

Gray's the rain & gray's the sky
when blades in graceless morning sigh
& weighing sink their alibis
in puddles drowned then grayed they die.
So profound, this grayness thine
yon burdensome dew drops of time
fall dripping from exalted climes
all slipping, halting, here combines
to make delay of swift decay
& break away from this dismay
with swaddled blankets overlaid
to hide the corpse— a wasted day.
Gray's the graves & gray the lies
which plagues of graceless mornings ply ✙

The dying are so damned unruly
when they've time to quit the stage.
Grin & bear it, says the sage
coz living's everyone's undoing.
I can't take it, shouts the tired
waiting for his fix to come.
He injects & then expires
nodding out. His pains are done.
The dying make such dull complaint
even making decent wages.
Grin & bear it, say the sages
coz living death's the state of saints.
We can't take it, quake the poor.
The sage's wisdom— slam the door ✝

A quartet of buskers

This magic moment
chapped lips sing close to thine
this tragic moment
the mourned commute of time ✢

I'm road-wearied & tired & I want to sleep
in the shade in the summer, in a hammock beneath
an oak tree whose canopy's arms far outreach
every glinting of sunlight. & in shadows complete
in the darkness & warmth of such humidity
which is brisk still, & cool, from the wind at one's feet—
I'll dream about nothing, as I dream now of sleep ✢

I scarcely slept within the city's heart
when I had first absconded from my town
which all my life I'd dreamed I would depart.
It was in the city I found
disturbances— that every passing sound
drifting thru my window from the streets
kept me awake & sweating through my sheets.
So often then I cured my ails in smoke
if I could not greet sleeping without fight.
I'd roll tobacco pinched with sandman's dope
& with a lighter tread the night
until I knew I'd sleep alright.
Across the avenue there was a park
where I would hold these vigils in the dark
& every time I left for this sojourn
I'd find a drunk Ukrainian on my stoop.
I called him chort, a russian word I'd learned
for pesky imps who like to spill your soup.
He enjoyed harassing & would whoop
"Plague of Flies!" at every passerby
but we'd formed an alliance, he & I

as every night I'd roll a cigarette
to give to chort for which he'd shake my hand
with concrete fingers. I can't forget
how I pitied that grotesque & lonesome man.
He told me of his life in his homeland
which he had left to seek fortunes abroad
& now his dreams had failed, as he was flawed
by love of drink, & accidents, & cops
& how his world was now this city block
where he had played for decades as a prop
for evil plagues of flies to pass & gawk.
I gathered this from months of scattered talks
as mostly he just bellowed gibberish
"Maybe yes, maybe no, maybe business
maybe snow, open doors, broken windows"
such were phrases he would chant
beneath that awning lit by ember's glow
where I listened to his nightly rants
& then I'd say "paka" & would scant ✢

Into my heart, a frozen knife
spawned from a virtual abyss.
What are these faint remembered sprites,
these bleeding cells, these pixels missed?

They are the rust of bygone worlds,
to which we'd once escaped
They are the dreams which once unfurled
from which we've now awaked ✢

The silence breaks. A hearty sneeze
asks for your attention please.
You're stuck with this soliloquy
because you left your headphones dumbly
somewhere you cannot return
but you see them curled up snugly
wrapped around your shaking fist
then dropped into amnesic mist
& now you're waiting for the Hudson
northbound up to where— Poughkeepsie?
where you've planned to see the stars
& make new friends in warmlit bars
to get real cozy—warm & tipsy
for a weekend— maybe more
& in the end— return, reborn
bereft of your malaise—you're sure
but anyways— this bum is speaking
& you are stuck with him, for now,
you're confident & sure & proud
that all your great plans will all work out
& he's got none of those- no hopes-
nothing but his tattered coats
that hide his bleak insinuations
in the camouflage of jokes—

"Good evening everyone- how are you?
Good I pray & wish you well—
I've got a sorry tale to tell
I'm sorry for it- sure as hell
forgive me everybody here
for forcing it upon a crowd
I know I know how you must feel
it wasn't long ago from now
that I passed people like myself
concerned with me & nothing else
& that is fine— it's fine— I thank you
I do not want your charity
I only feel compelled to share
the truth of everything— I've found—"
The train arrived— you didn't stay. ✣

Boss Boom rejected every gift.
He felt he hadn't earned them.
His Christmases were as austere
as a Puritan's.
& by virtue of his shrift
he was ushered to the helm
of Industry where down he peered—
Centurion
of office parks & malls
& statistics & baseball.
His corporate superiors
hadn't heard of him.
"No rather, it's the youth,
who disrespect our troops
who I believe most threaten me severely.
I'd bet a third of 'em are shits.
They want, but won't commit
to working for a pittance doled out yearly.

When I was young, well pal
I worked tons & saved somehow.
I thanked all of my employers so sincerely
for giving me the chance
to put on my business pants,
& tug my bootstraps firm & cavalierly.
I earned my pension, my retirement
& I find all this defilement
of my lifestyle to be nothing merely
but jealousy, & blame
of this noblest of man's games
for failures in your genes. You're thinking queerly.
& while I've got you here,
let me make this one thing clear
your time is mine, & I pay for it dearly.
So go my son, to work.
Be my apprentice, my wage serf.
Someday you'll be like me,
so don't be leery.
Someday you'll get promoted
& grow old, & weak, & bloated
& sup upon the blood of youth.
Be cheery!" ✧

My wood-pecking teeth & I chatter with violence
until I can calm, with heavy breath, cease
the electric convulsions, the skeleton's trembles

for a moment at least, I can bear it in silence—
'til the ice-arrow breeze breaks the tentative peace
& my quietist courage dissembles ✝

Headlights sweep the dusk across the sprawl.
A tide of blood is waning in the west.
Lulling us to dream within the thrall.
It's heroin or alcohol. I guess
these street-lamps could've seen much better days.
They're glowing orange— going faint.
They buzz like soda cans on cathode ray displays
pass smeared & warped in frozen rain—
still lifes of american decay
swollen in consumption, growing pained.
Thankfully I'm forced to look away
to southern highways promising escape
as swiftness carves this soul to streamlined shape ✛

Wisps with spiral emanations shake
from an ashy truck's sub-bass en route
to providence in early blizzard flakes
which helped me cover up the truth—
before we left I said that we'd arrived
safe with my friends, all safe inside
but we were far— so far from in the clear—
he was rolling- pinching knees to steer—
another one when last he only lit
& passed along so it was mine I guessed
so weightless stoned my eyes were razor slits
so unafraid of accidental death
he floored it where the other cars had wrecked
dumb— free—young— & criminally deft ✣

The life unplugged- man's dreaming analog
machines from scenes of future's he's forgot.
Imago mortis— cataleptic denouement
paralysis in horror at the ever-lingering-on.
The cloud of mind- inhuman epilogue
convening every theme of human thought.
Corpus mundi— septic babylon
the deity's apartness to atomic eidolons.
This all-four-blade plays guillotine tonight,
while perjury & prejudge execute
on qualified moralities of blood
charging the electric mobs in fright
& quantified beyond their sole compute.
Tonight the frogs of anguish croak for floods ✢

Peel your onions, pierce your veils,
question 'til your reason fails.
Disenchantment— render clear
the sovereigns who rule us here.
Tho' Space & Time are known to gloat
in realms abstract & far-remote
its Chaos & Contingency
who write decrees terrestrially.
Oh Space & Time are deaf & mute!
It's Circumstance who's Absolute!
Rolling dice & spinning wheels.
Place your bets, then fate's revealed,
& if you lose— "Who could've known?"
& if you win—"I told you so." ✢

The pastel luminescence
on the ceiling
of a passing room
three phantoms of senescence
& the feeling
of impending doom.

Oh evening's obsolescence-
these unsleeping
in the hospice tombed
three keeling convalescents
pleading pities
for their loss exhumed.

Where putrescence of subtlety
is dripping all to vein.
Munificence so suddenly
is stripped in squalls of pain.

Oh save me from these specters God—
I cannot here remain ✛

Listen how the word's elapsing-
axioms dissolving passions.
Action seizes. Thought's mere grasping
for the ruins in the ashes.
Lo! the Tower is collapsing,
Alexandria refashioned.
Listen how the word's elapsing—
axioms dissolved in passions.
Whence to where the soul Parnassian?
Heretofore gave worlds the lashing
nowadays, acts droll dispassion
in the guise of satisfaction.
Listen how the word's elapsing—
axioms dissolved to passions ✚

At least if you die
after burying gold
you can die believing
it will never be sold ✢

Time smolders in dispassionate drags
perched on the balconies of dread
where vacant lots & body bags
litter the concrete in your head
& moments drift away so slow
like ashes flicked after their glow
is snuffed out in the wind—
That's where a poem begins ✢

"Life is very long" whispers the wind
to the sidewalk slurried grey
Smoking a remorseful cigarette
"But once you had a friend"
a flurry of dismay
upon the fir you've slain—
in seasonal regret.
"How his branches green delighted
All colors dull. All is benighted."
You hide yourself. & now the rain
falls coldly faint on tannenbaum lane ✢

Marvel how the prince pretends
to ploy his faults to better ends:
"Lies? Well, if they're nobly told...
Crimes? Well, if they're nobly sold...
Pride? Well, if it's me who's scolding...
All's well held in my shareholdings.
Charities are well supplied.
They're tax exempt & certified.
My Greed? Oh please, be more adult.
My motivations? Hush. Results.
The bottom line— the numbers climb
& what is that if not divine?
What is done outside your sight?
I beg your faith. It's human, right
to err sometimes, in our ascent?
Why fixate on the detriments?
What's done is done— forgive, repent,
& while I have you here— your rent..." ✟

We've less resembled humans after all
since we have built this parallel abyss
wherein we can be lost amidst a thrall
of messages in bottles cast amiss.
For which of them can we claim to be ours?
& how could we know which of them we've stole?
or whether we're beneath the gaze of powers
when we ourselves are voyeurs of the shoals?
We never know. We shrug our shoulders. Laughing
at what a mess we've come to hold so dear.
& this predicament is lost in passing
our time which ebbs & flows like tears.
& if we somehow extricate our eyes
we'd simply disappear to all—& die ✢

What's this new terrain? Where have we fled
like waves succeeding waves upon this shore
crashing all us castaways aspread
as refugees to all the known-before?
I scarcely here approximate our fate.
Where we have drifted off's unrecognized
by any map or charter writ in time.
We're orphaned of all calendary dates,
all zones of jurisdiction, lawful tacts,
all heritage, traditions, human grasp
is powerless to claim its all-command.
Inquirers & Illusions rule the land.
Telemachus & Circe wedded here,
& since that day, the fog has never cleared ✢

I am the very model of a parasoical medium
I've information, masturbation, spectacle, & tedium.
I host the things you're thinking
& engross your mesocortical
with trivia & sentiments in garb phantasmagorical.
I'm very well acquainted, too,
with data merchandisable.
I command persuasion. Your profile's analyzable.
My datafarming engine reconceives you as commodity
an intersecting infonode in my network topography.

I'm very good at profiting off cyber-anthropology
although my scientific aim's for animal psychology.
My characterizations range from oligarch to plebeian.
I am the very model of a parasocial medium.

Aglow in mythic history, each brand is an Odysseus
lost in my Aegean Sea-- my Argus, you're oblivious!
You post your panegyrics & I profit off your industry.
It's all the same to me-- I'll even profit off your infamy!
I'm selling you engagements
with my operant conditioning.
Your psyche is the product
my conglomerate's partitioning.
When I sum all my figures
of which I've a whole zoology
I find I've got a lab for noospherical virology!

All diseased enchantments
are my Babylonic pharmakons.
All dramas I'll enhance
'til histrionic as the Parthenon.
In short, I'm psychoactive dissasociative delirium
I am the very model of a parasocial medium.

In fact, when I know everything you hate
& find outrageous
I can sell you fear itself— it's awfully contagious!
When such affairs as Billionaires,
of whom you should be wary at,
are pilfering the public purse,
you'll blame the Proletariat!
When I appraise the progress
that's been made in Propaganda—
"how beauteous... O Brave New World!"
said innocent Miranda
"Tis new to thee" Prospero said,
"you do yet taste some subtleties..."
the parasocial medium's the greatest of discoveries!

By curating the human need
for friendship & community
I'm capable of laundering PR beyond acuity
My psychogenic agency's half-bot & half-bacterium
I am the very model of a parasocial medium ✢

The out-wind's cold with whisperings of ghosts.
Your breath is plumed against a pall of fire
which dwindles in this realm, beyond all scope,
where lanterns of the intellect expire
& styluses of lightning pierce the night
with inks that set all emptiness alight,
revealing for a flash that all coheres,
then fast as it's disclosed, it disappears.
To rage against impermanence & death's
indicative, sometimes, of gallant hues
which fade away the same as all the rest
when thunderclap, apocalypse, pursues.
Eventually each grounded spine of man
is awestruck by divine command ✝

The sun is slanted, short & sulls.
There's less to do than even sleep.
Daylight dawdles, drear & dull,
& dreads inexorable defeat.
The moon is tucked behind a fog.
The air is dry & cold as death.
& nights are ever-thinning slogs
in walled confines of shrinking breadth.
The hearth's my only solace now
to thaw my frozen limbs. My hands
have long lain idle anyhow,
& fail to hear my heart's commands.
But a solstice bears in my direction
with presages of resurrection ✙

It's an ineffable adiaphoron
& we its humble eidolons
lift our limbs when pulled upon
by strings invisible, so sure
our poses proud or else demure
the masks it's fashioned for display—
yours scans overtly dismayed.
I sense it's this that you protest?
That the universal jests?
We want the spotlight on the stage
& tho we swell our chests
& tho we won't confess
when we've been bested at the game
the narrative remains
& so it shall refrain
entirely unchanged ✢

Each instrument of man is honed to kill,
but none is such a butcher as his Voice
with which he can dissever strength from will
& commandeer the bodies he employs.
       We've sharpened language still.
We've carved it into stone, & flesh, & warped
ourselves beneath all-pressing eyes. Who knows
the Truth without impurities absorpt?
Lacking this criterion, what flows
    but murk occluding all it has deposed?
Shadows pass as surfaces! The Deep!
Pansophia! Dread Anarch of Renown!
Which mysteries, within your waters, sleep?
& which have ineluctably been drowned?
      Where are your limits to be found?
Alphabattoir, the testament of men
who from the tips bleeding knives
        invented fountain pens ✞

Wouldn't it be nice if words would sanctify?
Well, some believe they do—
the same who claim to clear the skies
of clouds by mouthing "Blue!"
They've this cerulean clarity
advantaging their views—
a tribal jocularity sublimes the misconstrued ✝

On a corner, in a snowbound gutter
adorned in soot & stained with fumes,
I saw a songbird, half-aflutter,
half-alive, & half-displumed.
One of his legs was frozen, chained.
He sang to cars. The chilling rain
had done him in— but fell so soft
that morning mist's sedating loft...
I heard him hum his final melody,
a murmur-whispered bird-tongue threnody.
He sang of a translucent coat
that warmed him from the city's smoke
& numbed his starving nerves & soul,
& eased the pain of letting go ✢

The cat asks with eyes
damp in the anxious doorway
Shall I cross the line? ✢

THE WISDOM OF CLOW'N TZOO
A dialogue in the theme park of the world

I:
"What's found & is described is not what's found.
Its description is not it. Even this."
Warns the Sage.

"Nothingness is Everything itself
Everything in Nothing's born
Thus, Everything depends on Nothing
Nothing manifests Everything
Nothing observes Everything
Nothing desires Everything
Everything, from Nothing,
is Everything becoming Nothing."

But he is interrupted in his antinominous
testimonial by the Fool.

"This identity, the sage reveals, is this mysterious
or is our sage, like me, still foolishly delirious?

II:
The Sage says:
"If nothing knows something,
it knows nothing of itself.
If nothing knows nothing,
it knows all of itself.
Thus nothing knows nothing but itself
& what it knows is nothing & that's all.
Everything is nothing partly
& if something is nothing, it is
in the sum of everything
wholly nothing."

Therefore the Sage:
Exalts nothing-
Knows more than all in knowing nothing-
In doing nothing, does more than all-
In saying nothing, says more than all-
In being nothing, is more than all.

"& yet the Sage" says the Fool:
"Does not do nothing, & he says "I do not."
Does not see nothing, & he says "I do see not."
Does not say nothing, & he says "I say not."

III:
But I, the Fool
Do not exalt the Sage.
Do not exalt Everything & Nothing.
I ride the &. & the & is the Only Thing."

The Sage applauds & lauds the Fool's designs
there is a silence— then he testifies:

"The Fool lives in ignorance
knowing nothing of nothing
& only something of everything.

The Fool thinks not of nothing.
The Fool thinks not of everything.
The Fool thinks only of this something.
When he thinks he knows this something,
then he will also know
that he knows neither everything
nor nothing.

Because Everything is Nothing" intones the Sage.

"But I, the Fool know one thing, surely
If I know only one thing, I know this—
I know the Only Thing
to know is how to ride the &.

IV:
& the & is full of things—never empty.
Oh unfathomable multiplicity of things!
Drops in oceans,
Grains of sand,
Fruits in arbors,
Lives of man.
Oh ever new & ever reproducing!"
replies the Fool.
"But you know fractions of its size!
As beyond the &—everything & nothing lies.
& of these what have you to say?"
asks the Sage.

V:
"The & though ruthless
in its unceasing change."
the Sage says ruefully
"is in All diminished in its range
between Everything & Nothing.

A trivial thing this & of your design.
In the eyes of knowing this."

"The & tho' unyieldingly unwieldy.
Is wholly known simply. It is saying
Something's changing!
The more something moves, the faster it will go.
Nothing can't outpace it.
Everything lags behind it.
Such speaking is too slow.
Such thoughts do not change
like the dead— like the Sage!"
Says the Fool.

VI:
"The & can never die
it knows nothing of death.
The & sings of the root, & of the worm,
& of the bird, & of the eaten worm,
& of the roots that eat decaying birds.
The & of something's changing on
beyond everything & nothing's dead words
whatever is, there is, & more, & more.

VII:
The & will change something without audience.
It does something to garner Sage assent
then it courts his disdain.
Inconsistency— the only Foolish law
of something changing.

IIX:
& the & is like water.
Water births & drowns just the same.
& the & is like land.
Land births skulls & buries them again.
The pulse is like the &.
Speaking is like the &.
Walking is like the &.
Playing is like the &.
It is not dead nothing
nor dead everything.
All Becoming is the &."
Says the Fool.

"The vortex of everything becoming nothing
& nothing becoming everything again.
This is your only thing." Says the Sage.

IX:
"Here— the cup that runneth over
Here— the blade that cuts too thin
The best of riches can't be stolen:
Laughing at the Sage's chagrin."
Says the Fool.

X:
"Man & his environment
& how is there this separation?
Differences are but discernments.
& what of Sagely consternation?
Missing out on living action
the only thing!
for everything or nothing rather.
& what of all the time that's gone?
Shrugging it is satisfaction.
Nothing is not my concern.
Everything cannot be learned.
Can living action last for long?
Yes & No. Like any song."
Laughs the fool.

XI:
"A memory on Laserdisc—
that central hole's what did it in.
Times preserved are lost with vessels—
read mechanics made them live.
Level graveyards, build a mall—
this empty space can now be sold.
If nothing fills its vacant halls—
sell hypnagogic opiates.
Nothing remembered
becomes something again
but only on its return to becoming nothing.
Everything becoming Nothing.
Nothing to Nothing. The &
is the only thing between."
Says the Sage.

XII:
"Buy nothing
Sell nothing
Say nothing
Think nothing
or don't."

XIII:
"Buy everything
Sell everything
Say everything
Think everything
or don't."

XIV:
"There is only becoming.
Everything becoming nothing.
Nothing becoming everything."

"& the &."

XV:
The voices are tangled.
The fool becomes the sage.
The sage becomes the fool.

XVI:
lol — they say
in a delimited circle
with hands up in surrender
to ecstasy & fear
in the amusement park
between everything & nothing
on a rollercoaster
called "ampersand"

FAREWELL

Be gone. So long. Another book is done—
enchantments that grew feeding on my mind.
I've two excised & now my head feels clear
again— though I sense another & I fear
that I can't maintain in tranquil vacancy.
Another book interrupts my sleep.
I feel its tendrils twitching as it creeps
& lays a claim to every new conceit
with branches writhing serpentine— its bites
instilling me with poisons every night.
"What if we flip this image upside down
to fit the story of the town
that we've been writing since a child."
The daemon tempts. & I'm beguiled.

Made in the USA
Monee, IL
17 November 2020